What happens when you

BREATHE?

WHAT HAPPENS WHEN ... ?

What Happens When You Breathe?
What Happens When You Catch a Cold?
What Happens When You Eat?
What Happens When You Grow?
What Happens When You Hurt Yourself?
What Happens When You Listen?
What Happens When You Look?
What Happens When You Run?
What Happens When You Sleep?
What Happens When You Talk?
What Happens When You Think?
What Happens When You Touch and Feel?

Library of Congress Cataloging-in-Publication Data

Richardson, Joy.
   What happens when you breathe?

   (What happens when — ?)
   Bibliography: p.
   Includes index.
   Summary: Describes how we use air to build our bodies and to keep
ourselves alive and active.
   1. Respiration—Juvenile literature. [1. Respiration]   I. Maclean, Colin,
1930 -   ill.   II. Maclean, Moira, ill.   III. Title.   IV. Series: Richardson,
Joy. What happens when — ?
   QP121.R47   1986   612'.2   86-3728
   ISBN 1-55532-128-3
   ISBN 1-55532-103-8 (lib. bdg.)

This North American edition first published in 1986 by
Gareth Stevens, Inc.
7221 West Green Tree Road   Milwaukee, Wisconsin 53223, USA

First published in the United Kingdom by Hamish Hamilton Children's
Books with an original text copyright by Joy Richardson.

Typeset by Ries Graphics, ltd.
Series editor: MaryLee Knowlton
Cover design: Gary Moseley
Additional illustration/design: Laurie Shock

What happens when you

BREATHE?

Joy Richardson

pictures by
Colin and Moira Maclean

introduction by
Gail Zander, Ph.D.

Gareth Stevens Publishing
Milwaukee

... a note to parents and teachers

Curiosity about the body begins shortly after birth when babies explore with their mouths. Gradually children add to their knowledge through sight, sound, and touch. They ask questions. However, as they grow, confusion or shyness may keep them from asking questions, and they may acquire little knowledge about what lies beneath their skin. More than that, they may develop bad feelings about themselves based on ignorance or misinformation.

The *What Happens When ... ?* series helps children learn about themselves in a way that promotes healthy attitudes about their bodies and how they work. They learn that their bodies are systems of parts that work together to help them grow, stay well, and function. Each book in the series explains and illustrates how one of the systems works.

With the understanding of how their bodies work, children learn the importance of good health habits. They learn to respect the wonders of the body. With knowledge and acceptance of their bodies' parts, locations, and functions, they can develop a healthy sense of self.

This attractive series of books is an invaluable source of information for children who want to learn clear, correct, and interesting facts about how their bodies work.

GAIL ZANDER, Ph.D.
CHILD PSYCHOLOGIST
MILWAUKEE PUBLIC SCHOOLS

The moment you were born
you took a deep breath.
You have gone on breathing ever since.
You do it without thinking.

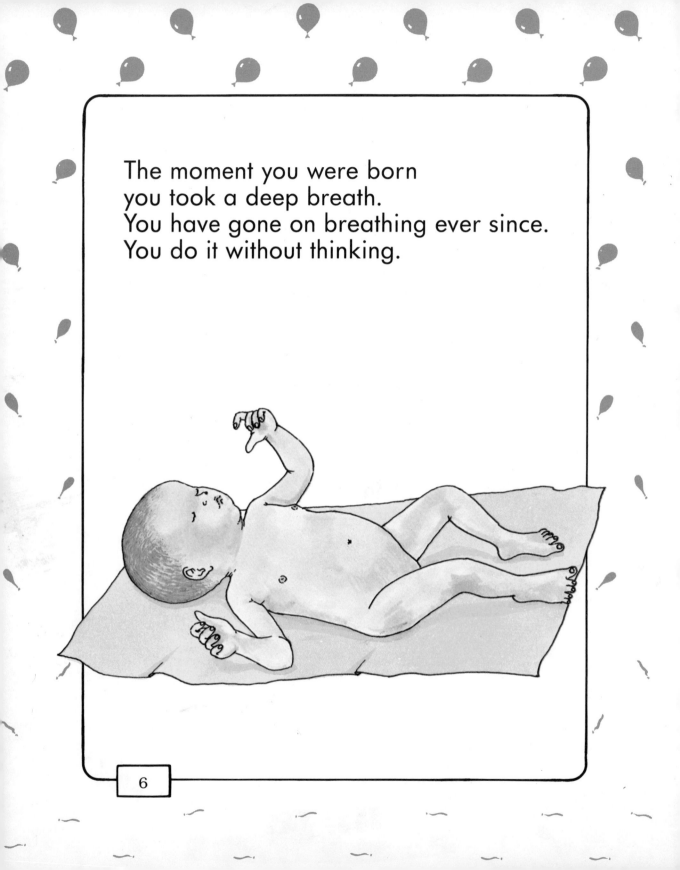

Watch a minute go by
on a clock or a watch.
Count how many times you breathe
in one minute.

You breathe every minute
of every day of your life.
That's a lot of breaths!

You cannot live without
air to breathe.

You cannot see air,
but it is all around you.

Put water in a bowl you can see through.
Turn a jar upside down.
Push it straight down into the water.
What is keeping the water out?

Can you let the air out now
so that the water can get in?

You cannot see air,
but it fills up empty spaces.

Your nose is made for breathing.
It is wet and warm inside.
Cold air begins to warm up
when it goes through your nostrils.

Inside your nostrils
there are little hairs
and slimy stuff called mucus.
The hairs and the mucus
catch any dust in the air.

You can breathe through
your mouth, too.

Sit quietly.
Are you breathing through your nose
or your mouth?

Run in place as fast as you can.
How are you breathing now?

You breathe through your mouth
if you need a lot of air quickly
or if your nose is blocked.

Your mouth hole
and your nose holes
join up at the back of your mouth.

The air goes down the windpipe
in your throat.

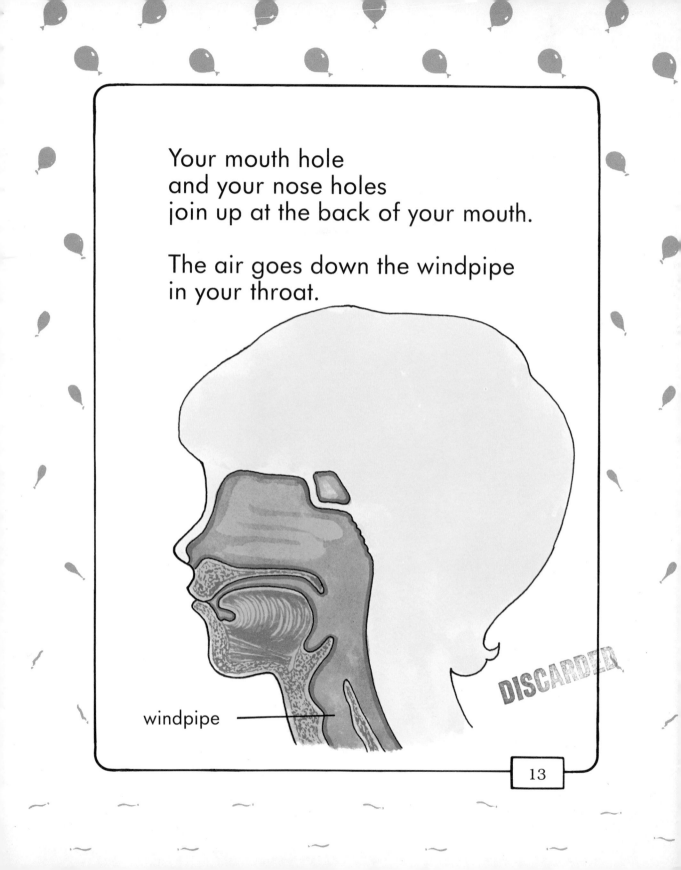

windpipe

13

Can you feel your windpipe
down the front of your neck?
The top part is your voice box.
It needs air to make it work.

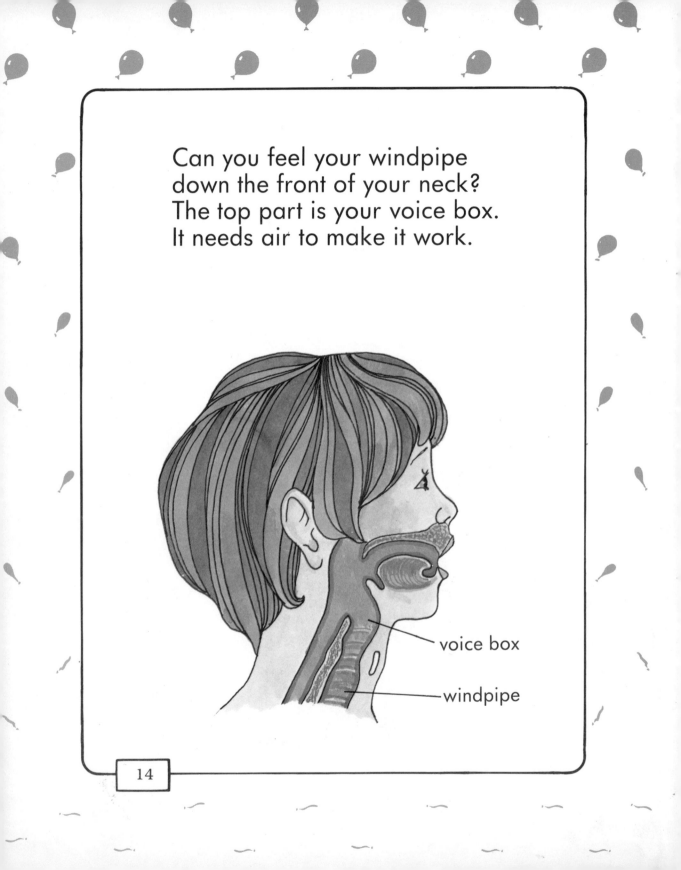

voice box

windpipe

Inside your chest
the windpipe splits into two.
The air goes down the pipes
into your lungs.

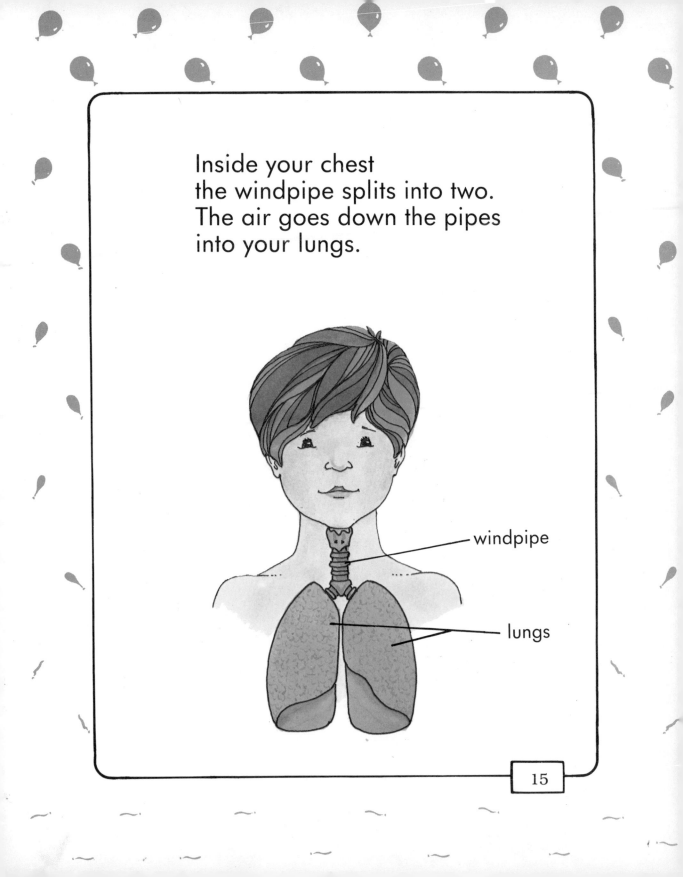

windpipe

lungs

You have two lungs.
They fill your chest.
Your lungs are soft and spongy.

Your ribs go around them
like a cage.
Can you feel your ribs?

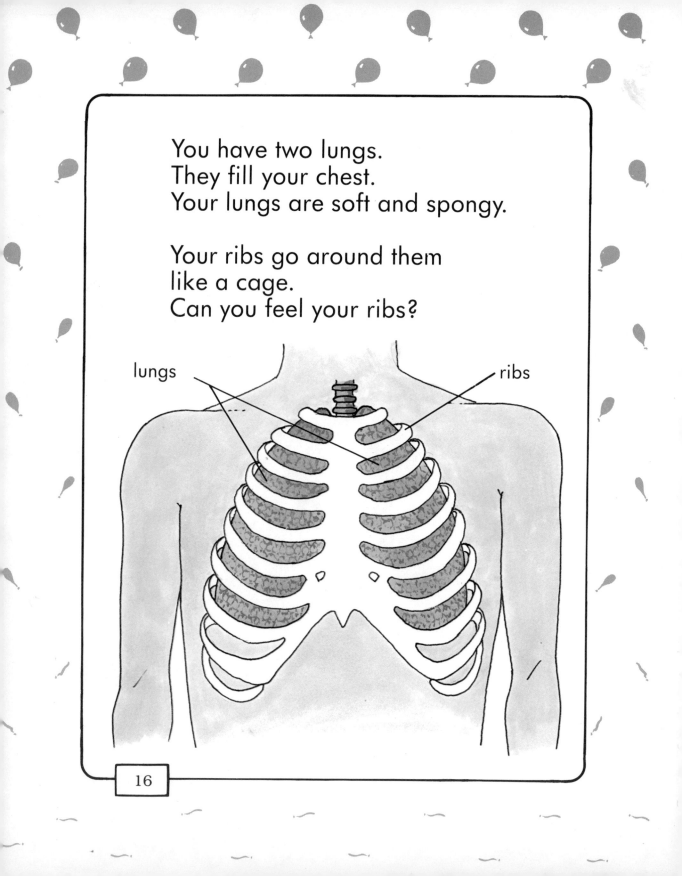

lungs

ribs

There are muscles between your ribs.
Under your lungs,
there is a big muscle
called the diaphragm.
(You say it like this: die-a-fram.)

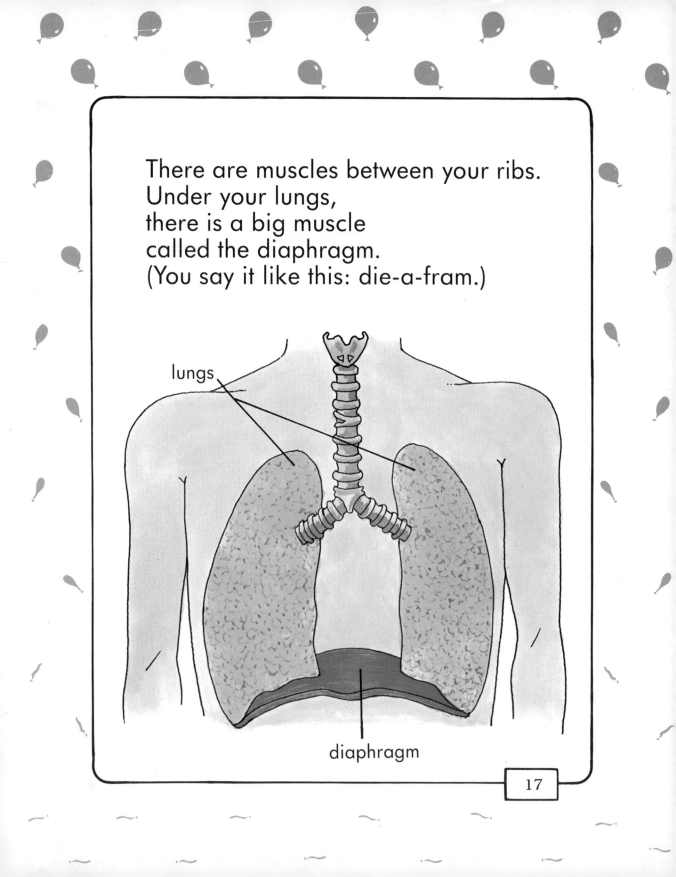

lungs

diaphragm

When you breathe in,
the muscles tighten.
Your chest pulls out
to make more space for your lungs.

When you breathe out,
the muscles relax.
Your chest gets smaller again.

breathe in   breathe out

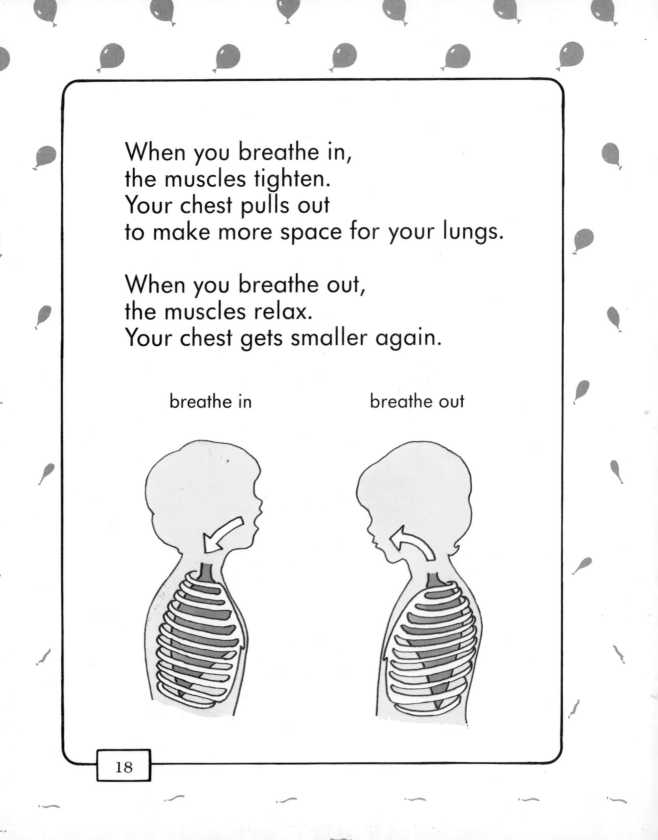

Measure around your chest
with a tape measure
or a piece of string.
Take a deep breath in.
How much bigger
is your chest now?

Inside your lungs, little pipes
carry the air to millions
of tiny air bags.
When you breathe in,
the tiny bags fill with air.
Your lungs get bigger.

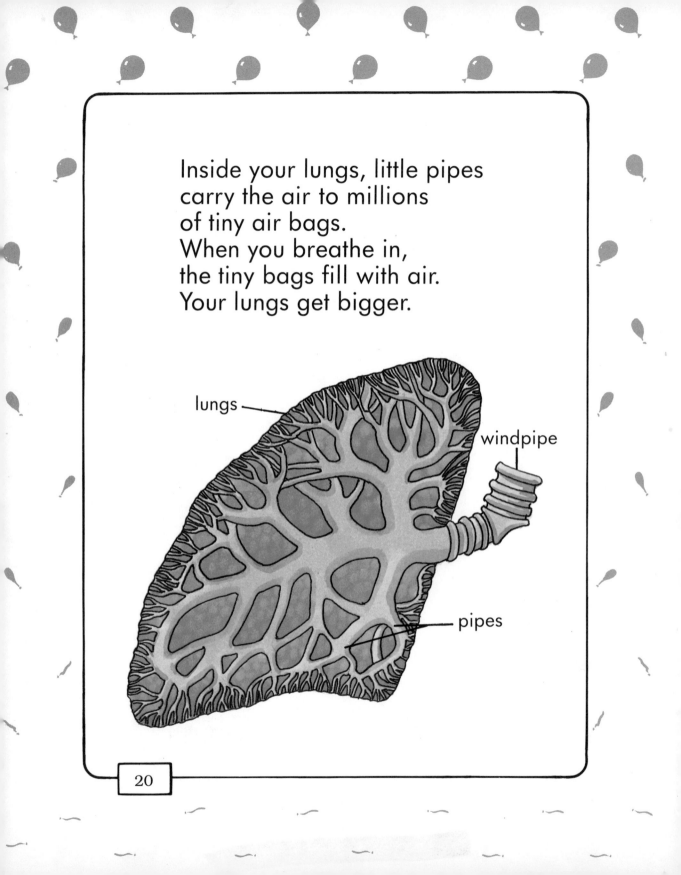

lungs

windpipe

pipes

Fasten plastic bags to the ends
of two plastic straws.
Put the other ends in your mouth.
Breathe out and in.
Watch the bags fill up and empty
like a pair of lungs.

Your body only needs
the part of the air called oxygen.

Thin tubes carry blood around
all the tiny air bags.
Oxygen from the air
mixes with the blood.

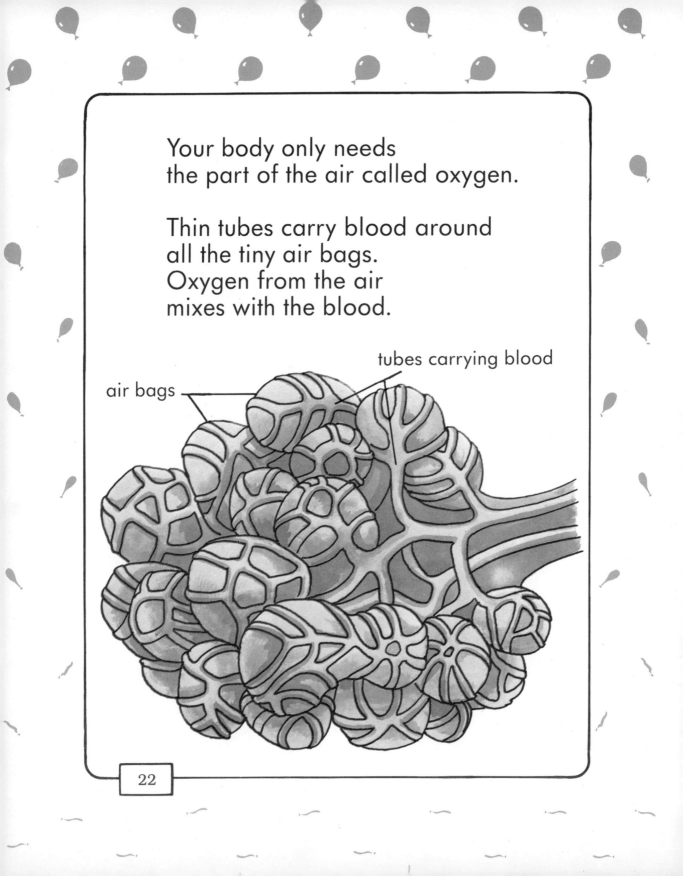

air bags

tubes carrying blood

The rest of the air
stays in your lungs
until you breathe out.

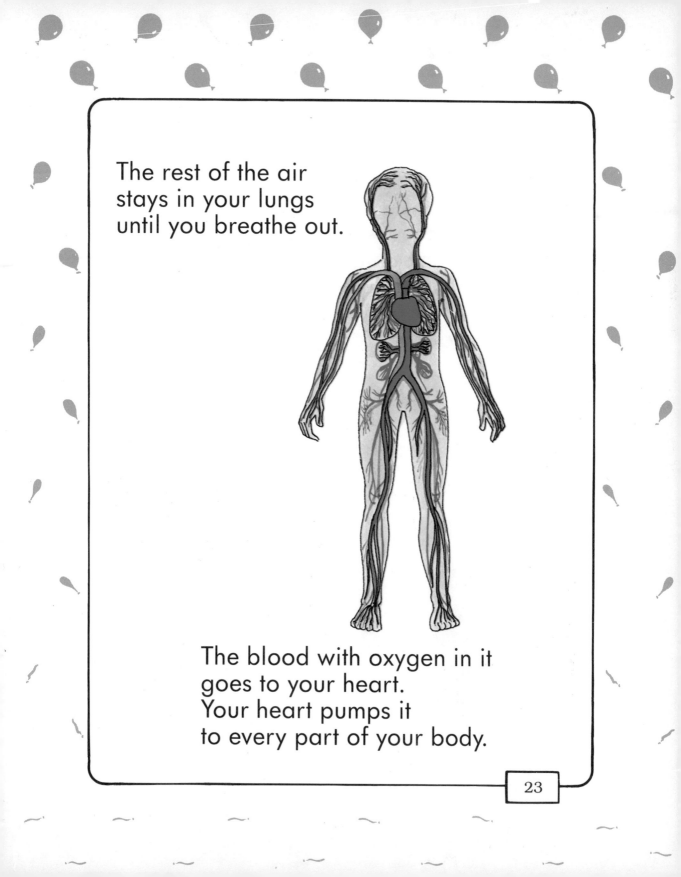

The blood with oxygen in it
goes to your heart.
Your heart pumps it
to every part of your body.

Oxygen turns the food
in your body into energy.

You breathe lightly
when you are asleep.
When you are using a lot of energy,
you breathe harder.
You need more oxygen.

Your heart pumps the blood
back into your lungs again.
The old used air goes back
into the tiny air bags.
The blood collects oxygen
from the new air.

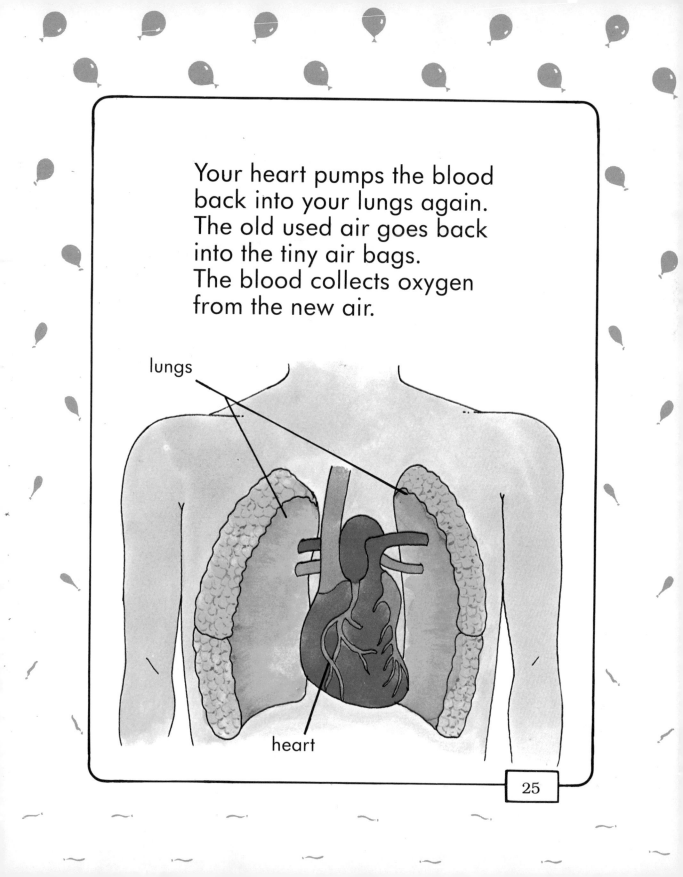

lungs

heart

When you breathe out,
the old warm air is pushed
out of your lungs.
It goes back up your windpipe
and out your nose or mouth.

Find a large jar you can see through.
Put it under water in the sink.
Turn the jar upside down,
keeping the water in.
Put one end of a piece of tubing
under the mouth of the jar.
Blow down the other end.

Make a mark on the jar to show
how much air came out of your lungs
in one breath.
Let your friends have a turn.

You may not be able to see air.
But it's nice to know that it's there!

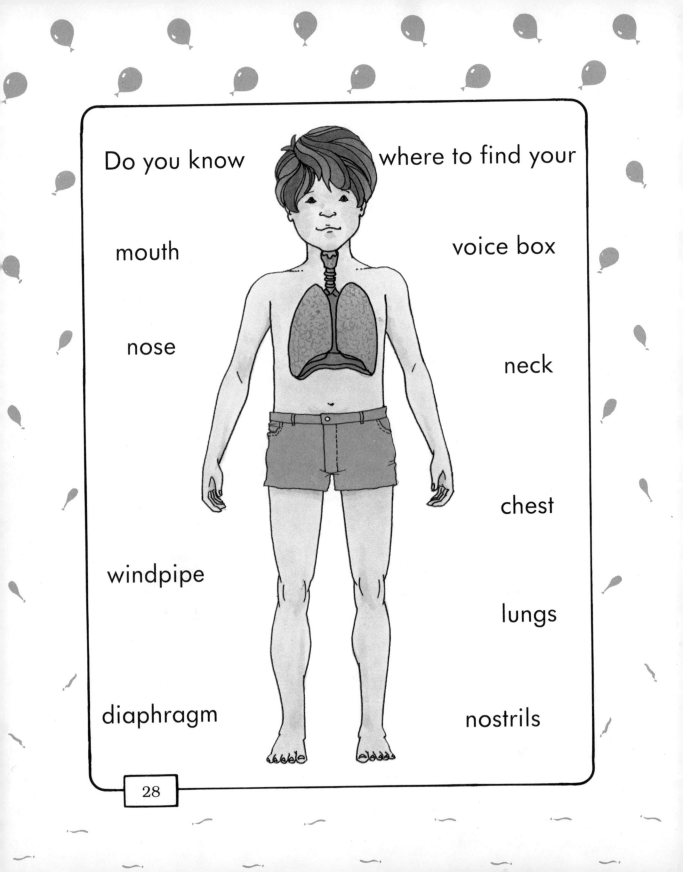

Do you know where to find your

mouth

voice box

nose

neck

chest

windpipe

lungs

diaphragm

nostrils

How Does That Happen?

Did you find all these things to do in *What Happens When You BREATHE?* If not, turn back to the pages listed here and have some fun seeing how your body works.

1. Count how many times you breathe in one minute. (page 7)
2. See how air fills up empty spaces. (page 9)
3. How do you breathe when you do different things? (page 12)
4. Find your windpipe. (page 14)
5. Find your ribs. (page 16)
6. Measure your chest when you breathe. (page 19)
7. Make some lungs from two plastic bags and two straws. (page 21)
8. See how much air comes out of your lungs. (page 27)
9. Find the parts of your body that help you breathe. (page 28)

More Books About Breathing

Listed below are more books about what happens when you breathe. If you are interested in them, check your library or bookstore.

Air. Brandt (Troll)
Amazing Air. Smith (Lothrop, Lee & Shepard)
Beginning to Learn about Smelling. Allington/
    Cowles (Raintree)
Follow Your Nose. Showers (Crowell)
From Head to Toes: How Your Body Works.
    Packard (Simon & Schuster)
The Lungs and Breathing. Ward (Franklin Watts)
Oxygen Keeps You Alive. Branley (Crowell)
Smells: Things to Do with Them. Puffin Editors
    (Puffin)
Taste and Smell. Catherall (Silver Burdett)
Your Nose and Ears. Iveson-Iveson (Franklin
    Watts)

Where to Find More About Breathing

Here are some people you can write away to for more information about what happens when you breathe. Be sure to tell them exactly what you want to know about. Include your name and address so they can write back to you.

American Lung Association
1740 Broadway
New York, New York 10019

Public Affairs Pamphlets
381 Park Avenue South
New York, New York 10016

Index